CONTENTS

INTRODUCTIO

The Top 100 Interesting & Fun Facts for Smart Kids is a captivating book that takes readers on an extraordinary journey through the world of ancient civilizations, animals, nature, inventions, sports, explorers, space, astronomy, human body, science experiments, natural phenomena, and environmental conservation. The book explores the mysteries of Ancient Civilizations, the diverse life on Earth, inventions and gadgets, sports and athletes, and the mysteries of the universe. It also delves into the world of sports and athletes, showcasing the skills and determination of athletes who push the limits of human potential. The book also explores the mysteries of the human body, revealing the intricacies of our organs, systems, and senses.

The book also features fun and mind-boggling science experiments, bringing science to life and leaving readers in awe of the natural world. The book encourages readers to embrace the call of environmental conservation, learning how to protect and preserve our planet for future generations.

The Top 100 Interesting & Fun Facts for Smart Kids is a must-read for young explorers, allowing them to unlock the secrets of the past, present, and future.

Happy Reading To All..
and **Thank you** for your purchase and
I most importantly for **Trusting us!**

ANCIENT CIVILIZATIONS

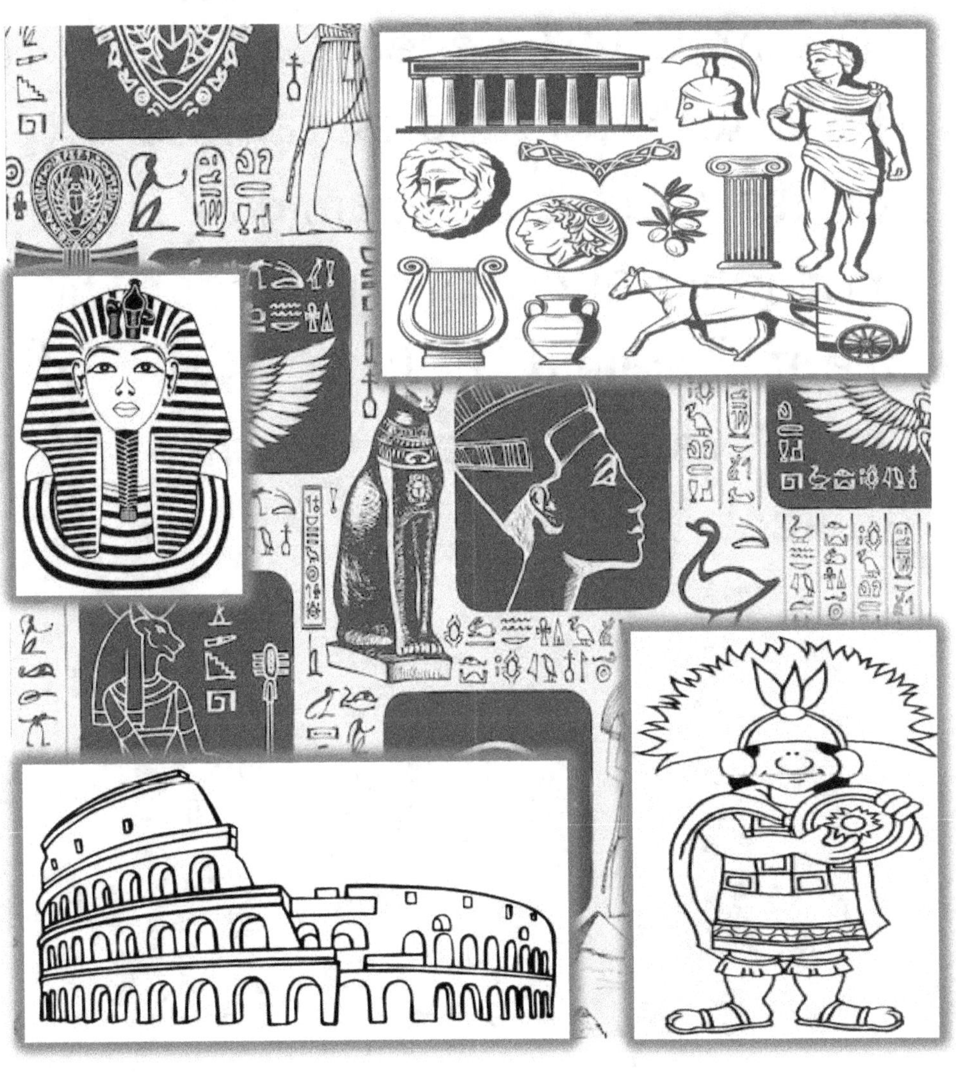

Ancient Egypt 

Ancient Egypt developed along the Nile River and is famous for its majestic pyramids, pharaohs, and hieroglyphics. The Great Pyramid of Giza is one of the Seven Wonders of the Ancient World.

Ancient Greece

Ancient Greece was the birthplace of democracy, and its philosophers, such as Socrates, Plato, and Aristotle, shaped Western philosophy. The Olympic Games also originated in ancient Greece.

Ancient Rome

Ancient Rome was a powerful empire that spanned several continents. The Romans built impressive structures like the Colosseum and aqueducts. They also introduced the concept of representative government.

Maya Civilization

The Maya civilization thrived in Mesoamerica and is known for its advanced writing system, magnificent pyramids, and intricate calendar. They were skilled astronomers and mathematicians.

Inca Empire

The Inca Empire was the largest pre-Columbian civilization in the Americas. They built the famous city of Machu Picchu high in the Andes Mountains and had an extensive road network.

Indus Valley Civilization

he Indus Valley Civilization flourished in the Indian subcontinent around **2500** BCE. They had well-planned cities with advanced drainage systems and a script that is yet to be fully deciphered.

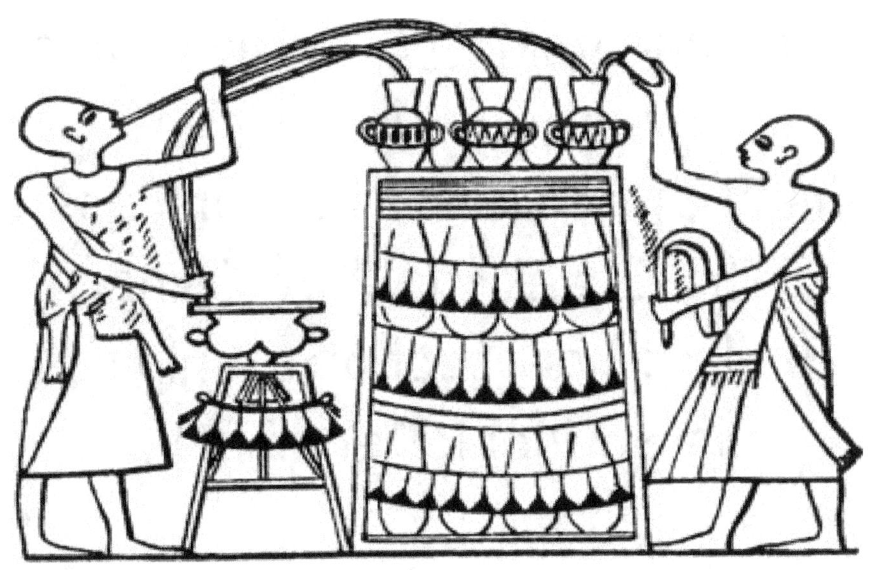

Ancient China

Ancient China gave the world
inventions like paper,
gunpowder, and the compass.
The Great Wall of China,
built to protect the empire,
is an iconic landmark.

Mesopotamia

Mesopotamia, often called the cradle of civilization, was located between the Tigris and Euphrates rivers. It is known for its city-states, such as Babylon and Ur, and the development of writing.

Ancient Persia

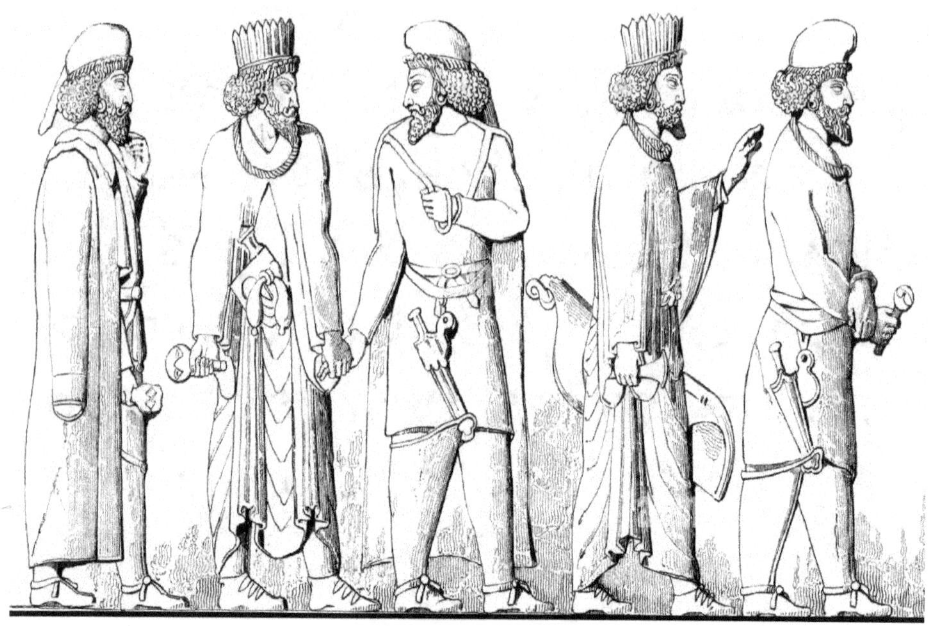

Ancient Persia, also known as the Achaemenid Empire, was one of the largest and most influential empires in history. King Cyrus the Great is remembered for his tolerance and respect for different cultures.

Aztec Empire

he Aztec Empire thrived in Mesoamerica and was known for its capital city, Tenochtitlan. They had a complex social structure, unique art and architecture, and a rich mythology.

ANIMALS AND NATURE

Biodiversity

Biodiversity refers to the variety of plant and animal species on Earth. Did you know that Earth is home to millions of different species, ranging from tiny insects to enormous whales?

Camouflage

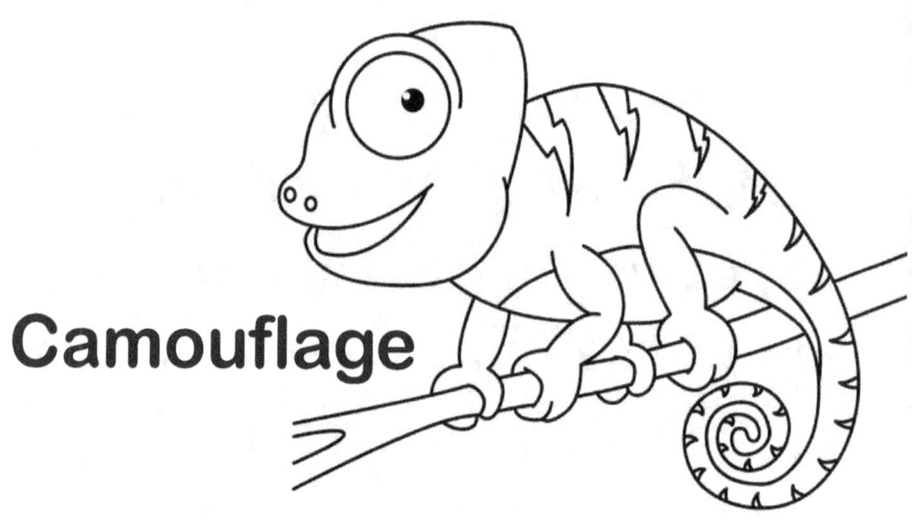

Many animals have the remarkable ability to change their appearance to blend in with their surroundings. This is called camouflage, and it helps them hide from predators or sneak up on prey.

Migration

Migration is the seasonal movement of animals from one place to another. For example, birds migrate to warmer regions during the winter to find food and suitable habitats.

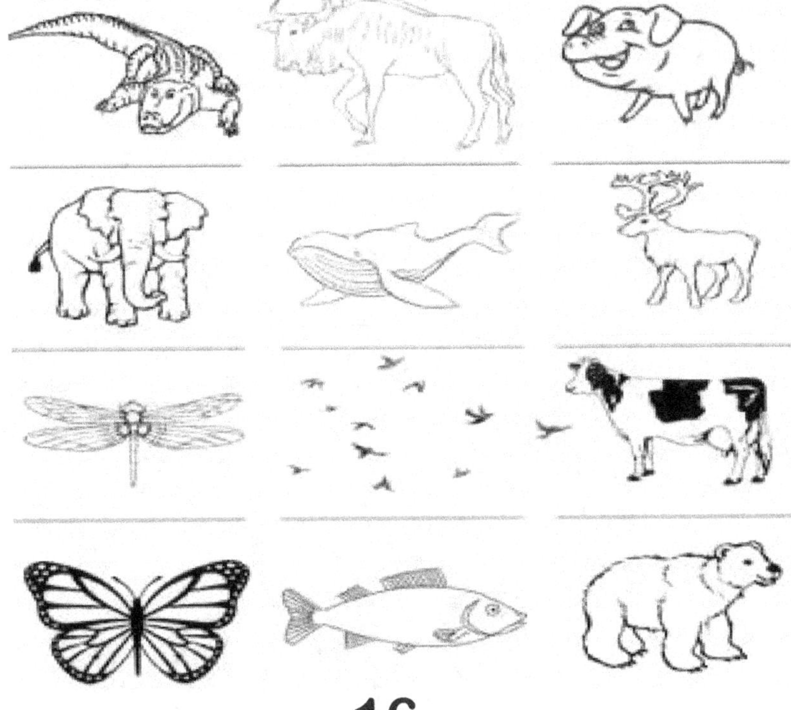

Ecosystems

An ecosystem is a community of living organisms (plants, animals, and microorganisms) interacting with their environment. Rainforests, oceans, and deserts are examples of different ecosystems.

Endangered Species

Some animal species are in danger of extinction due to factors like habitat loss and poaching. Learning about endangered species helps us understand the importance of conservation efforts.

Animal Adaptations

Animals have unique adaptations that help them survive in their environments. For instance, a giraffe's long neck enables it to reach leaves high up in trees.

Pollination

Pollination is the process of transferring pollen from the male part of a flower to the female part, allowing plants to reproduce. Bees, butterflies, and birds are common pollinators.

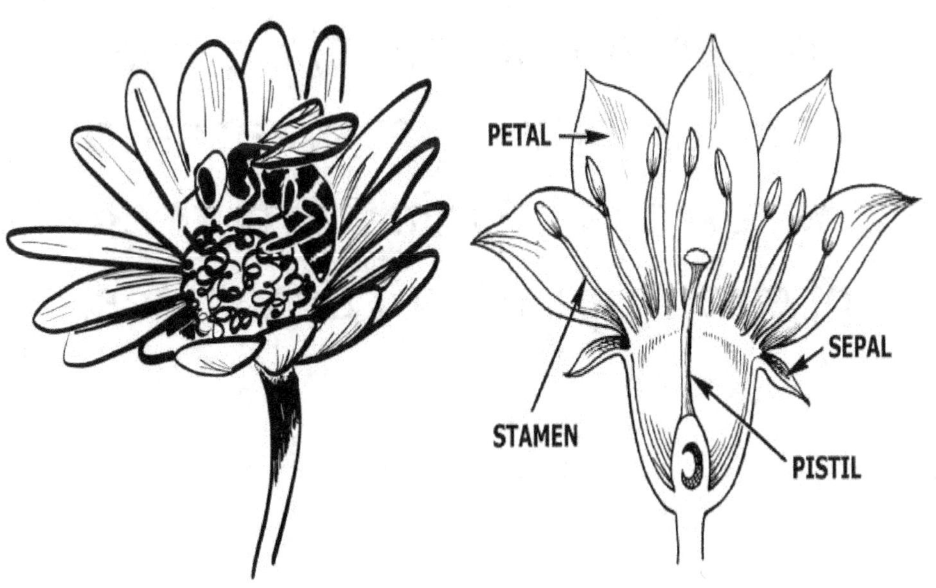

Food Chains

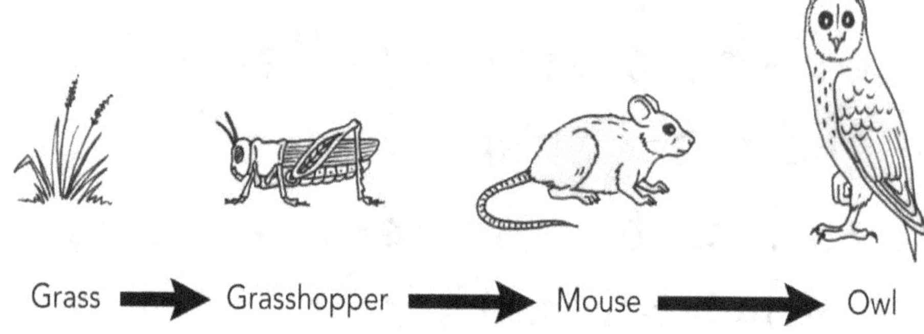

A food chain shows the flow of energy from one organism to another. For example, plants are eaten by herbivores, which are then preyed upon by carnivores.

Marine Life

The world's oceans are teeming with fascinating marine life, from colorful coral reefs to majestic whales. Exploring the underwater world introduces us to a diverse array of creatures.

Conservation

Conservation involves protecting and preserving natural resources and habitats. Teaching kids about conservation encourages them to be responsible stewards of the environment.

INVENTIONS AND GADGETS

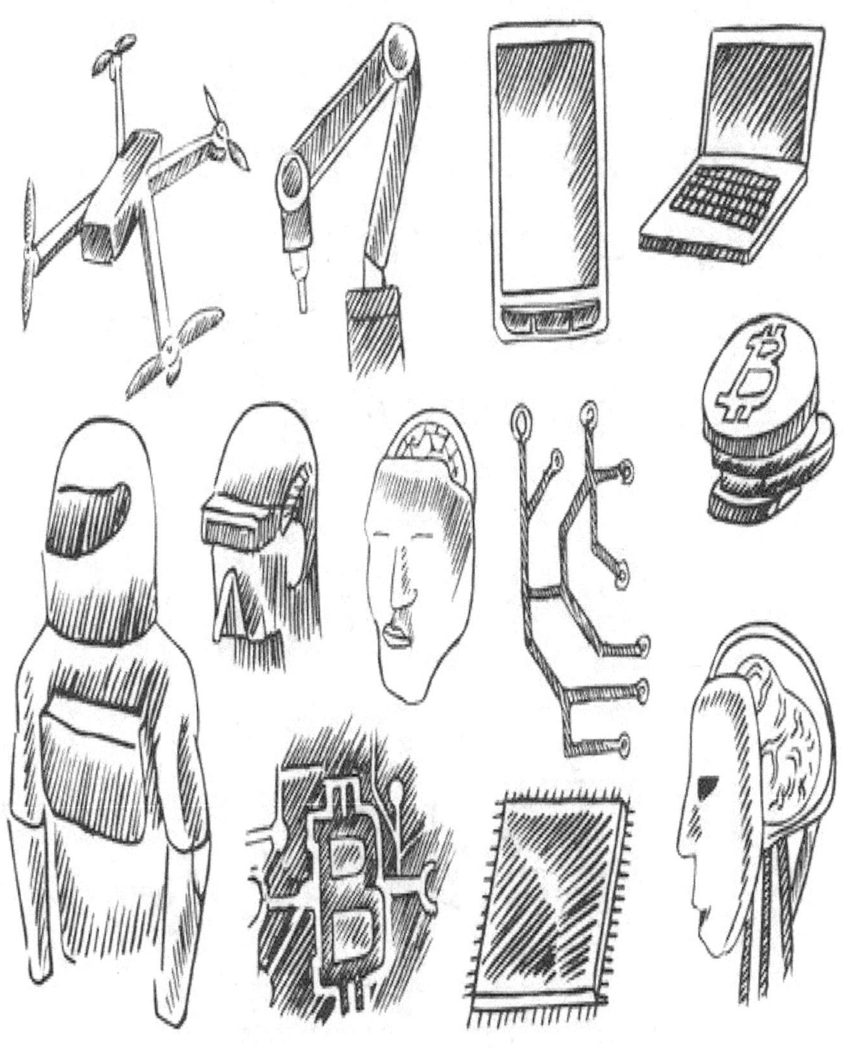

The Internet

The internet is a global network of computers that allows people to connect and share information. It has revolutionized communication, learning, and entertainment.

Computers are devices that process and store information. They have become an essential part of our lives, from personal computers to laptops and tablets.

Smartphones

Smartphones are mobile devices that combine the functions of a phone, computer, camera, and more. They have transformed the way we communicate and access information.

Electricity

Electricity powers many of our inventions and gadgets. It was harnessed for practical use in the late 19th century and has since become vital for lighting, heating, and powering various devices.

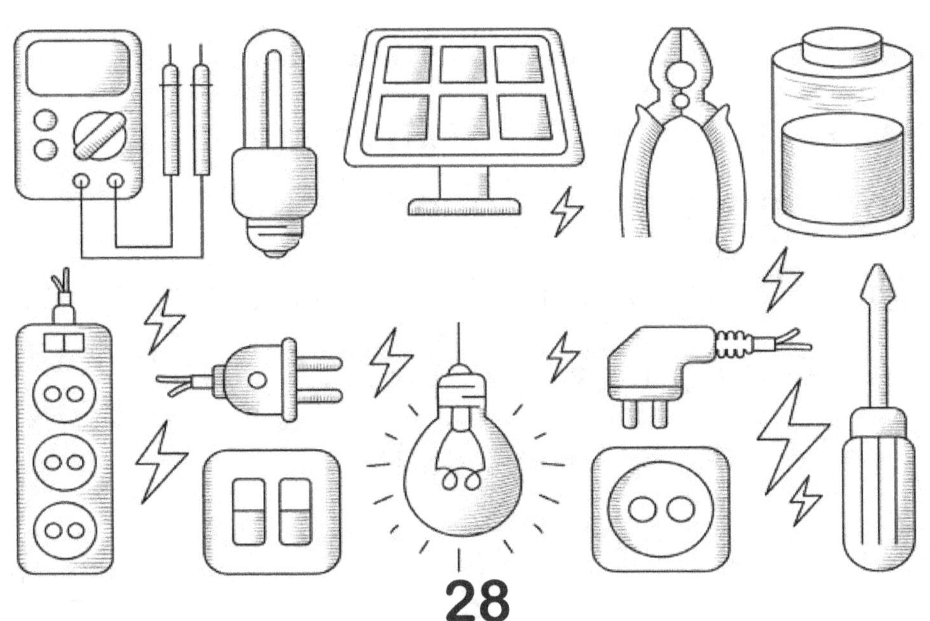

Robotics

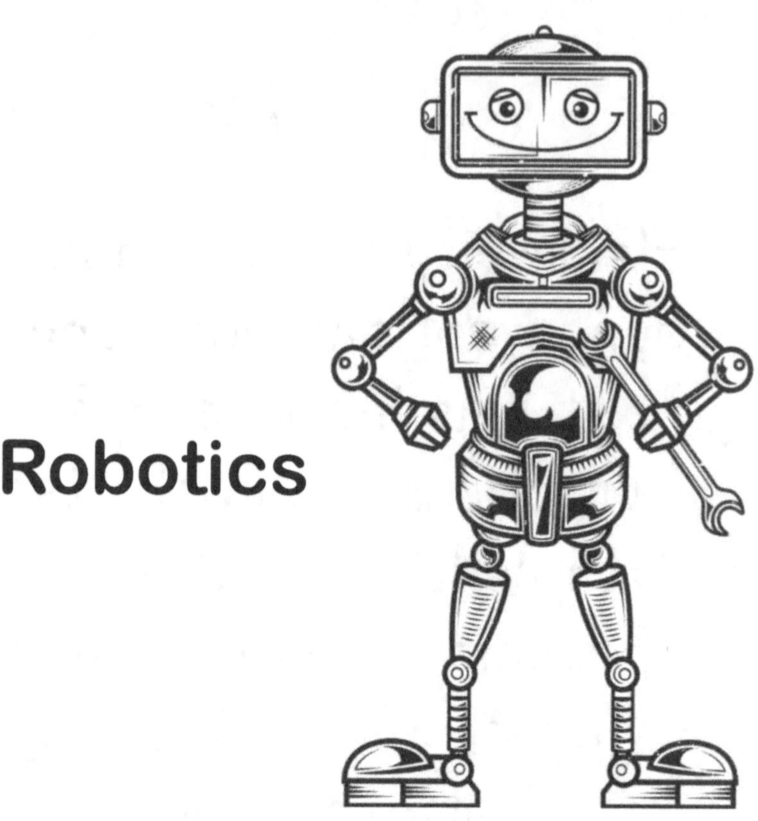

Robotics involves the design and creation of robots. Robots are machines programmed to perform tasks and can be found in industries, exploration, and even as companions.

Printing Press

The printing press, invented by Johannes Gutenberg in the 15th century, allowed for the mass production of books. It played a crucial role in spreading knowledge and shaping the modern world.

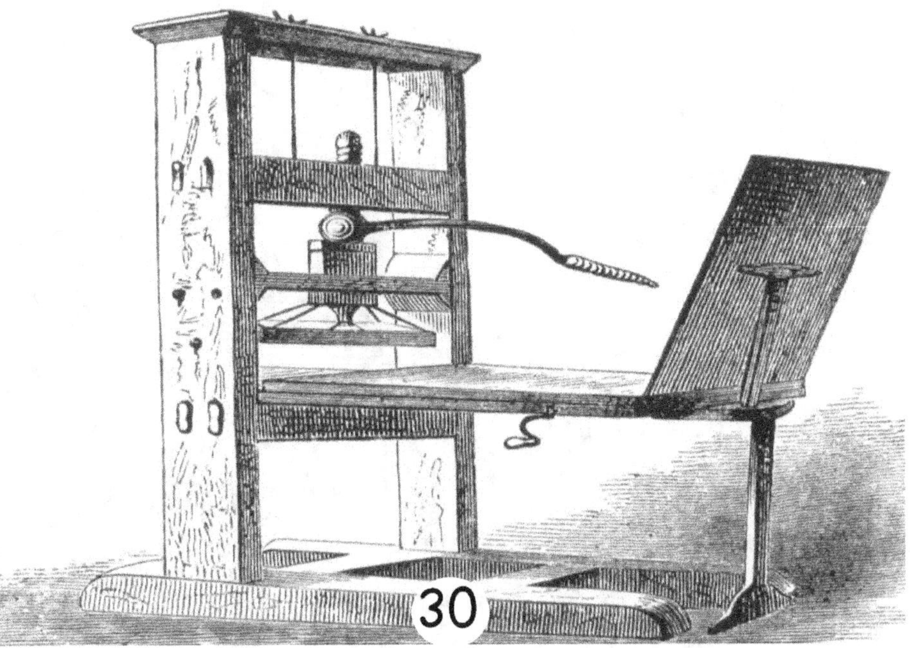

Cameras

Cameras capture and preserve moments in the form of photographs. From early film cameras to digital cameras and smartphone cameras, they have transformed the way we document our lives.

The first cameras were developed in the 19th century

Transportation

Inventions like cars, trains, airplanes, and bicycles have revolutionized transportation, making it faster, more convenient, and accessible to people around the world.

Video Games

Video games provide interactive entertainment and have evolved from simple arcade games to immersive experiences on consoles, computers, and mobile devices.

Renewable Energy

In response to environmental concerns, inventions focused on renewable energy, such as solar panels and wind turbines, have emerged as sustainable alternatives to traditional energy sources.

SPORTS AND ATHLETES

Olympic Games

The Olympic Games bring athletes from all over the world together to compete in various sports. The modern Olympics started in 1896 and take place every four years.

Soccer

Soccer, also known as football in many countries, is the most popular sport globally. It is played by more than **250** million people worldwide.

Soccer was invented in England in the 19th century.

Usain Bolt

Usain Bolt, from Jamaica, is considered the fastest man in the world. He holds multiple world records in sprinting and has won numerous Olympic gold medals.

Serena Williams

Serena Williams is one of the greatest tennis players of all time. She has won multiple Grand Slam titles and is known for her powerful and dynamic playing style.

Michael Phelps

Michael Phelps is the most decorated Olympian in history. He has won a total of 23 Olympic gold medals in swimming.

Gymnastics

Gymnastics is a sport that combines strength, flexibility, and grace. Athletes perform routines on various apparatus, such as the balance beam, uneven bars, and vault.

Basketball

Basketball is a popular sport played worldwide. It was invented by Dr. James Naismith in 1891, and the National Basketball Association (NBA) is one of the most-watched professional sports leagues.

Simone Biles

Simone Biles is an exceptional American gymnast known for her incredible skills and dominance in the sport. She has won multiple Olympic gold medals and is considered one of the greatest gymnasts of all time.

Cricket

Cricket is a bat-and-ball sport played in many countries, especially in the United Kingdom, Australia, India, and South Africa. It is known for its strategic gameplay and international rivalries

Jesse Owens

Jesse Owens was an African-American track and field athlete who won four gold medals at the 1936 Berlin Olympics. His achievements broke racial barriers and inspired many.

45

AMAZING ADVENTURES AND EXPLORERS

Marco Polo

Marco Polo was an Italian explorer who traveled to China in the 13th century. His book, "The Travels of Marco Polo," introduced Europe to the wonders of Asia and inspired future explorations.

47

Roald Amundsen

Roald Amundsen was a Norwegian explorer who became the first person to reach the South Pole in 1911. He led a successful expedition and beat his rival, Robert Falcon Scott, in the race to the pole.

Mount Everest

Mount Everest is the highest peak in the world, located in the Himalayas. Many adventurers dream of climbing it, and Sir Edmund Hillary and Tenzing Norgay were the first to reach its summit in 1953.

Amelia Earhart

Amelia Earhart was an American aviator and the first woman to fly solo across the Atlantic Ocean. She set numerous aviation records and inspired generations of female pilots.

Lewis and Clark

Meriwether Lewis and William Clark led the famous Lewis and Clark Expedition in the early 19th century. They explored the western territories of the United States and documented their discoveries.

Jacques Cousteau

Jacques Cousteau was a French explorer and marine conservationist. He co-developed the Aqua-Lung, a breathing apparatus that allowed divers to explore the ocean depths, and produced popular documentaries about marine life.

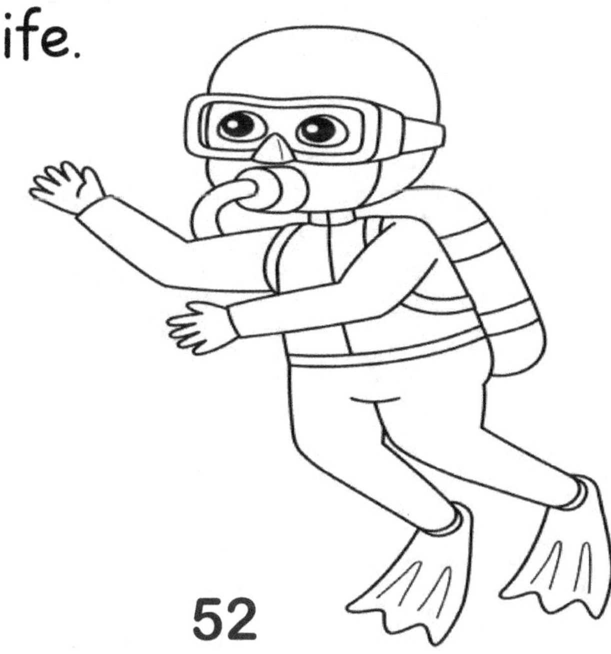

The Silk Road

The Silk Road was an ancient network of trade routes connecting Europe and Asia. It facilitated cultural exchange and the trading of goods, such as silk, spices, and precious metals.

Sacagawea

Sacagawea was a Shoshone woman who accompanied Lewis and Clark on their expedition. She served as an interpreter and guide, playing a vital role in their successful journey.

Sir Ernest Shackleton

Sir Ernest Shackleton was a British explorer who led expeditions to the Antarctic. His most famous expedition was the ill-fated Endurance expedition, where he displayed remarkable leadership and determination to save his crew.

Edmund Hillary and Tenzing Norgay

Sir Edmund Hillary and Tenzing Norgay were the first climbers to successfully reach the summit of Mount Everest in 1953.

SPACE AND ASTRONOMY

Our Solar System

Our solar system consists of the Sun, eight planets, and various other celestial objects. The planets, in order from the Sun, are Mercury, Venus, Earth, Mars, Jupiter, Saturn, Uranus, and Neptune.

The Moon

The Moon is Earth's only natural satellite. It orbits around the Earth and takes about 27.3 days to complete one revolution.

The Sun

The Sun is a star located at the center of our solar system. It is so massive that it accounts for about 99.86%of the total mass of the solar system.

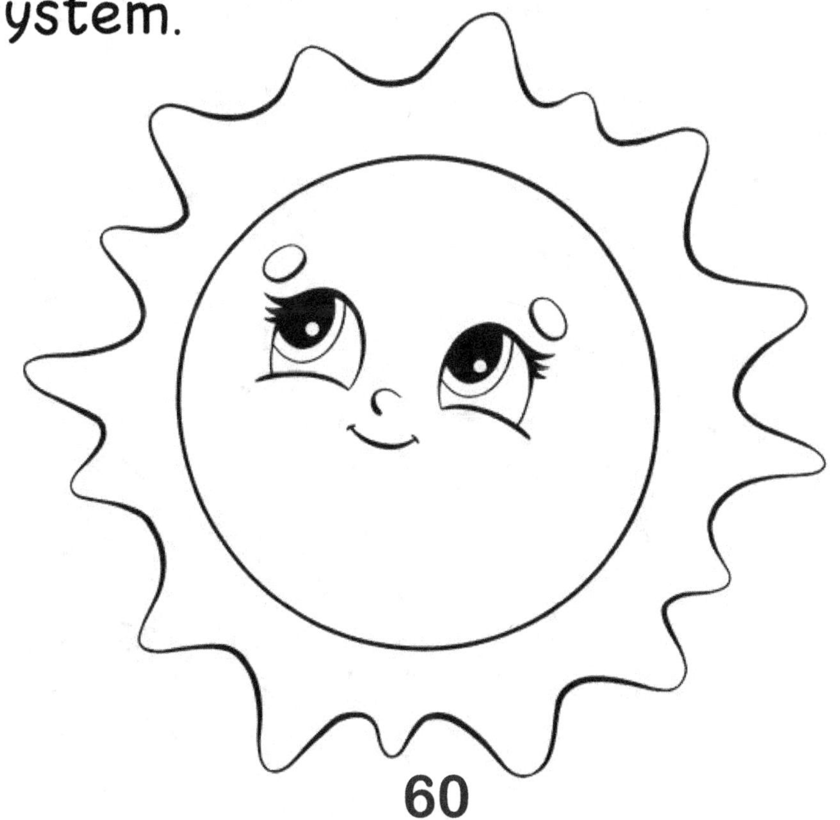

Black Holes

Black holes are regions in space with extremely strong gravitational forces. They are formed when massive stars collapse. Their gravity is so intense that nothing, not even light, can escape them.

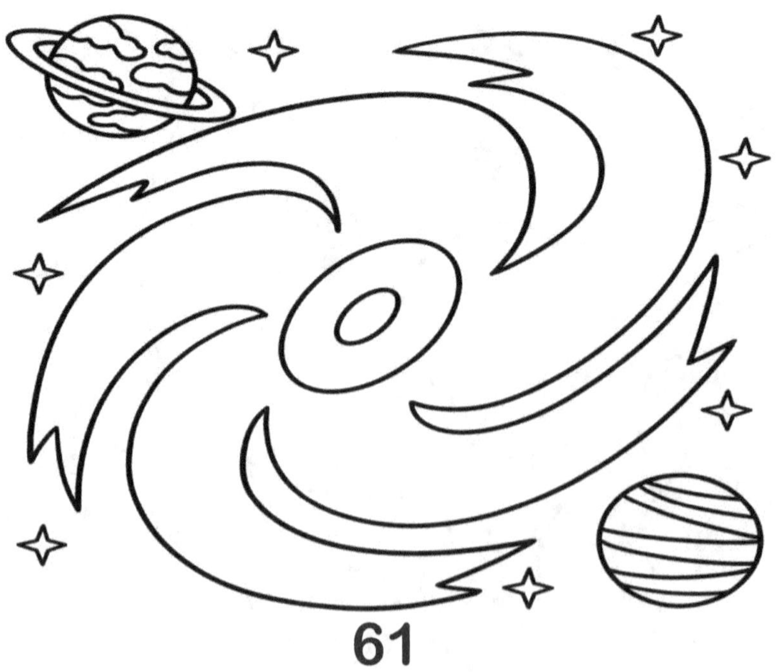

Galaxies

Galaxies are vast collections of stars, gas, and dust held together by gravity. The Milky Way is the galaxy we belong to, and it contains billions of stars.

Astronauts

Astronauts are highly trained individuals who travel to space to conduct scientific research, explore, and work on space missions. They live and work aboard spacecraft, such as the International Space Station (ISS).

Space Probes

Space probes are robotic spacecraft sent to explore space and gather information about celestial bodies. They have provided us with valuable data about planets, moons, asteroids, and comets.

The Big Bang

The Big Bang is the scientific theory that explains the origin of the universe. It suggests that the universe began as an extremely hot and dense singularity, then expanded, cooled down, and continues to expand to this day.

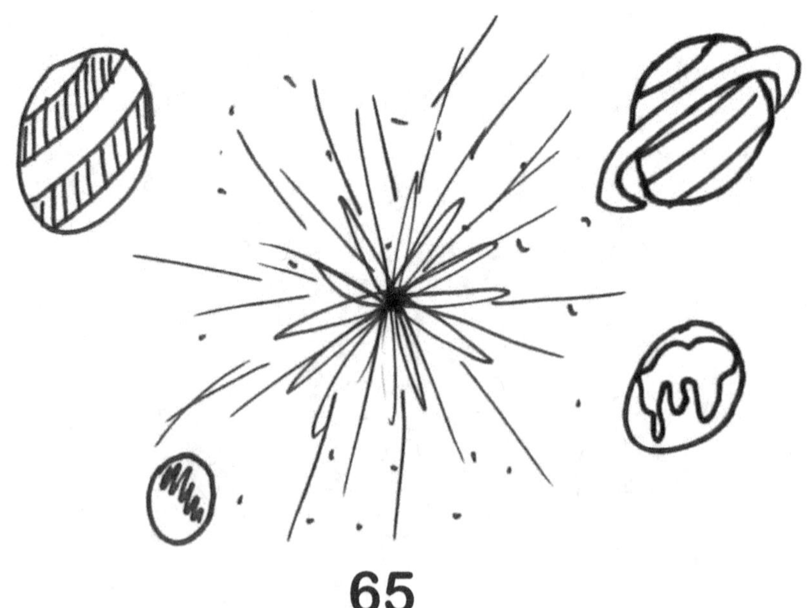

Exoplanets

Exoplanets are planets that orbit stars outside our solar system. Scientists have discovered thousands of exoplanets, some of which may have conditions suitable for life.

Constellations

Constellations are patterns formed by stars in the night sky. People from different cultures have named and associated stories with these patterns for thousands of years.

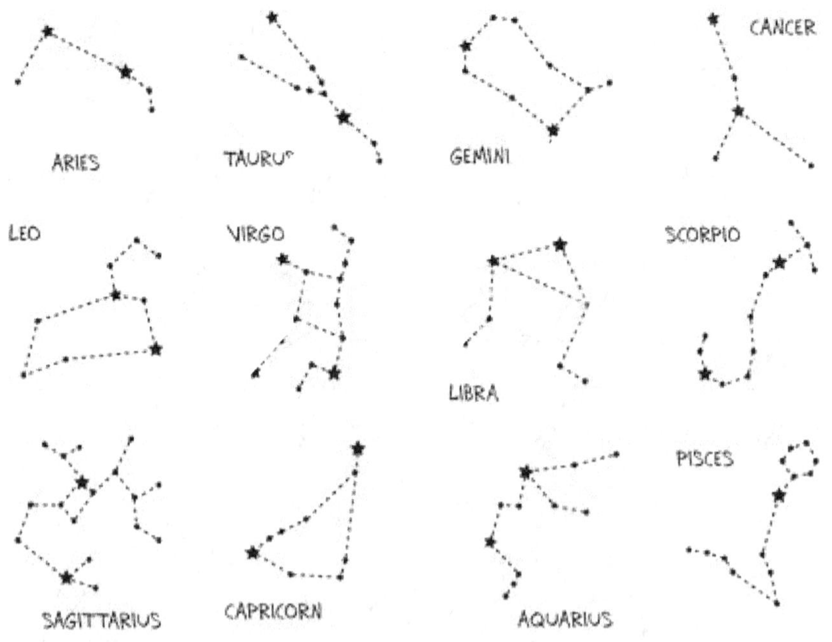

FASCINATING FACTS ABOUT THE HUMAN BODY

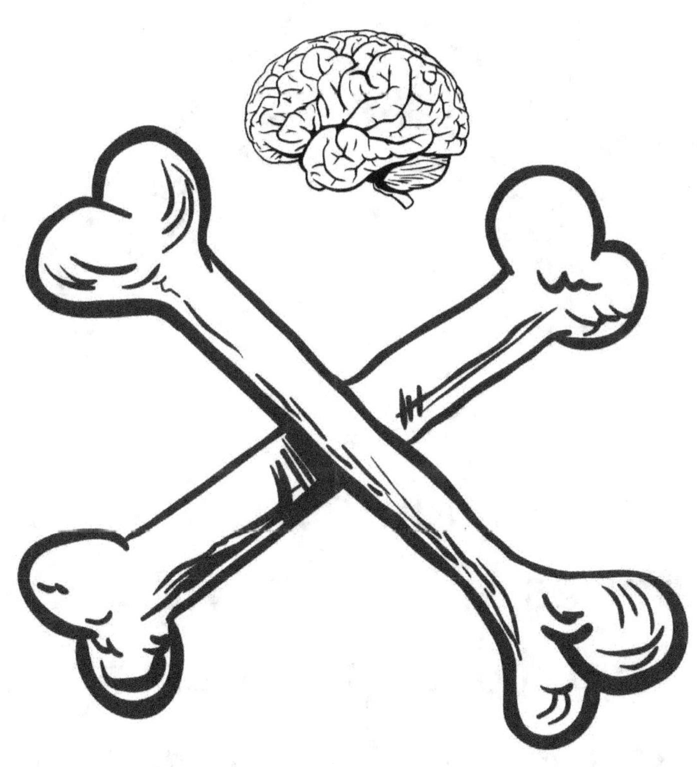

Bones

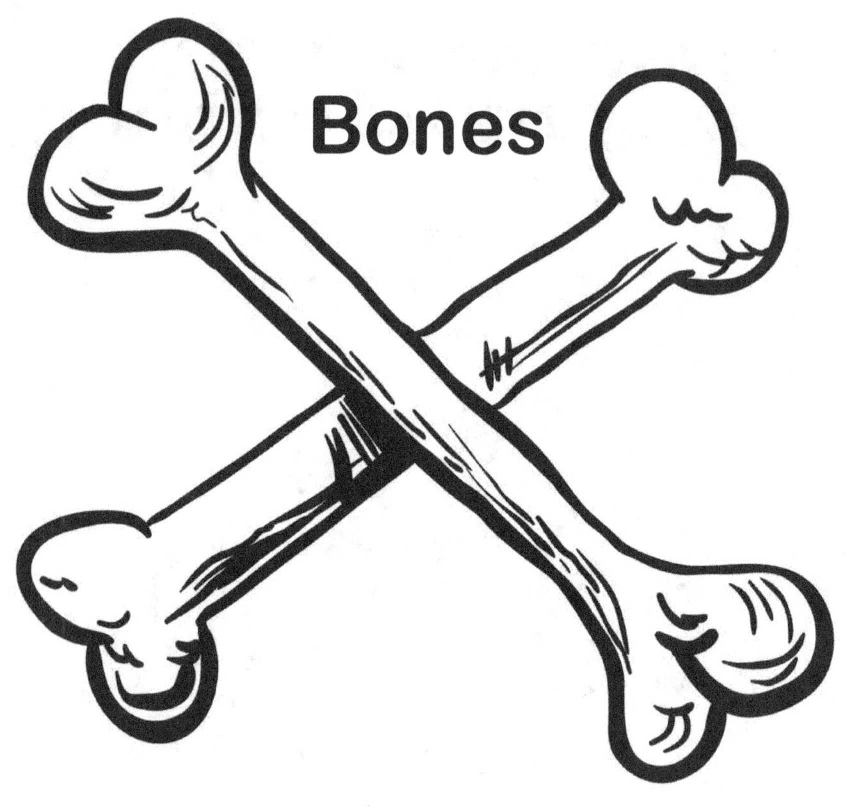

The human body has 206 bones. They provide structure, protect organs, and allow for movement.

Taste Buds

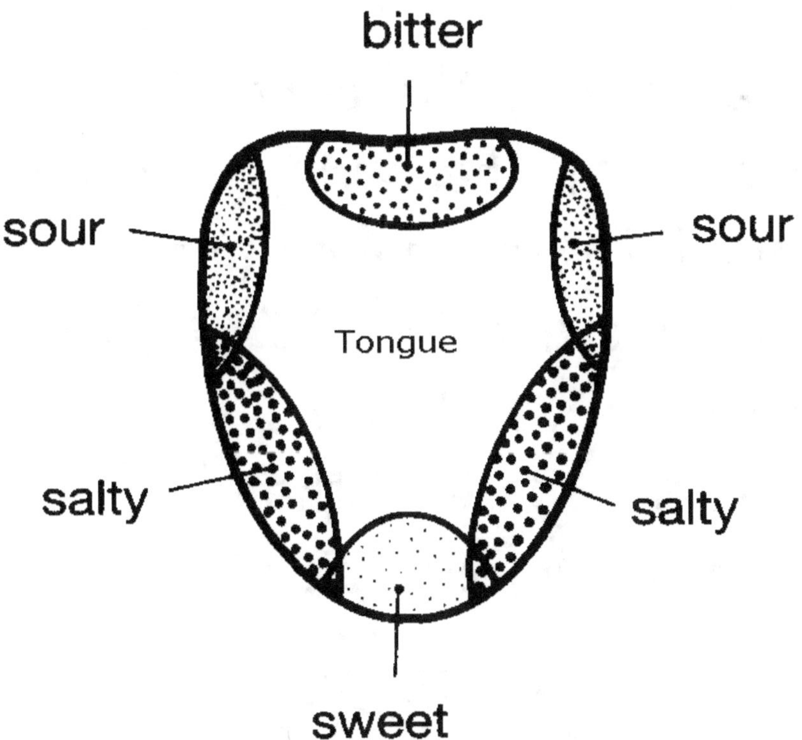

The average person has around 10,000 taste buds on their tongue. They help us experience various flavors like sweet, sour, salty, and bitter.

70

Brain

The brain is the control center of the body. It weighs about three pounds and contains around 100 billion neurons, which are specialized cells that transmit information.

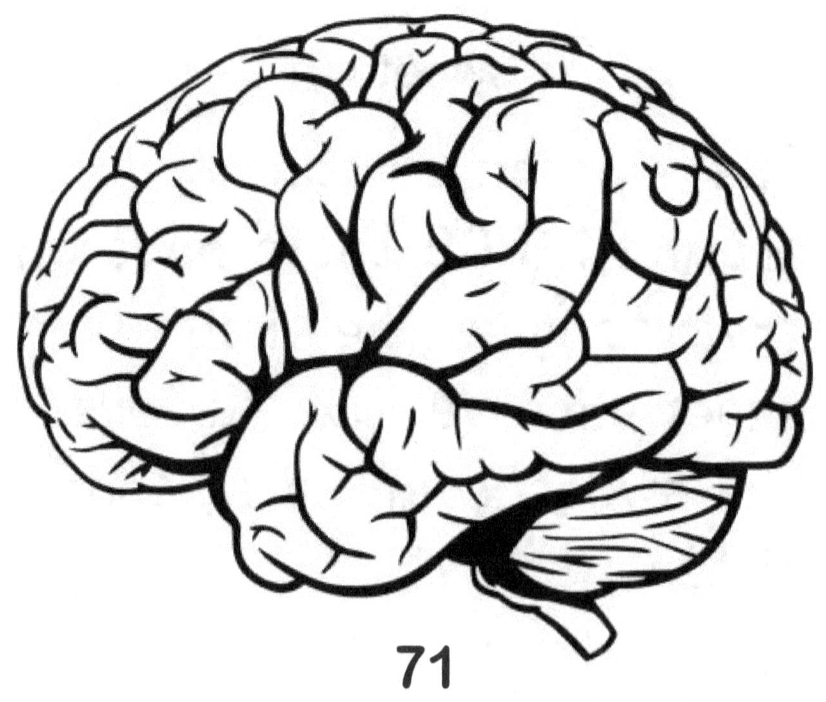

Digestive System

The digestive system helps break down food and absorb nutrients. The small intestine, despite its name, is the longest part of the digestive tract, measuring about 20 feet in length.

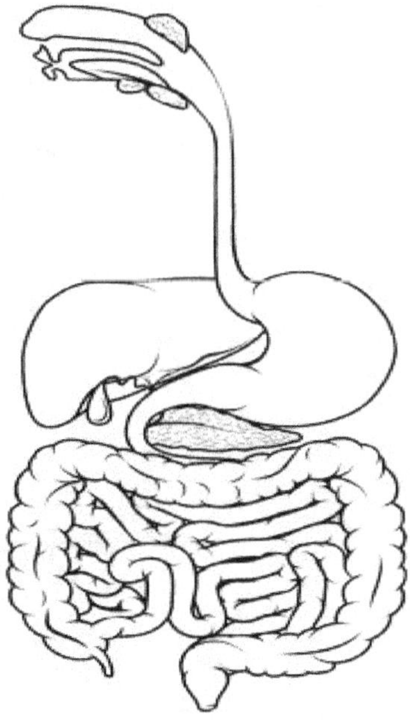

Heart

The heart pumps blood throughout the body. It beats about 100,000 times a day and can continue beating even if it's separated from the body.

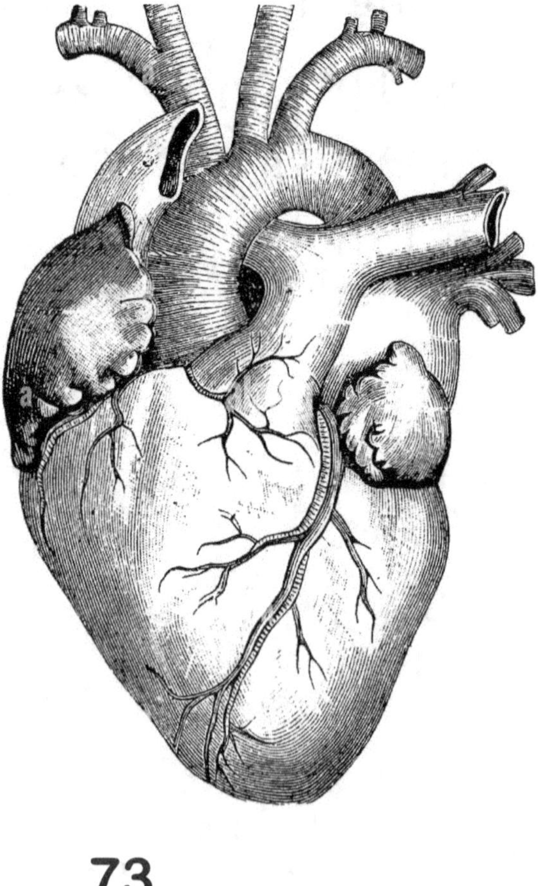

Lungs

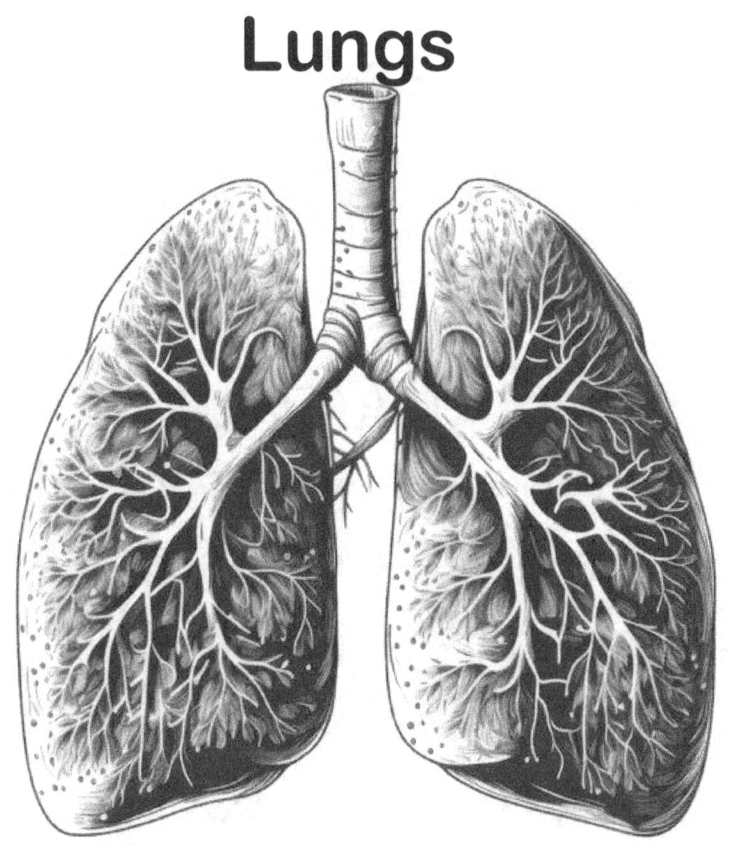

The lungs allow us to breathe. In an average adult, the lungs contain around 600 million tiny air sacs called alveoli, providing a large surface area for oxygen exchange.

Skin

The skin is the body's largest organ. It acts as a protective barrier, regulates body temperature, and contains sensory receptors for touch, temperature, and pain.

Muscles

There are over 600 muscles in the human body. They help us move, maintain posture, and generate body heat.

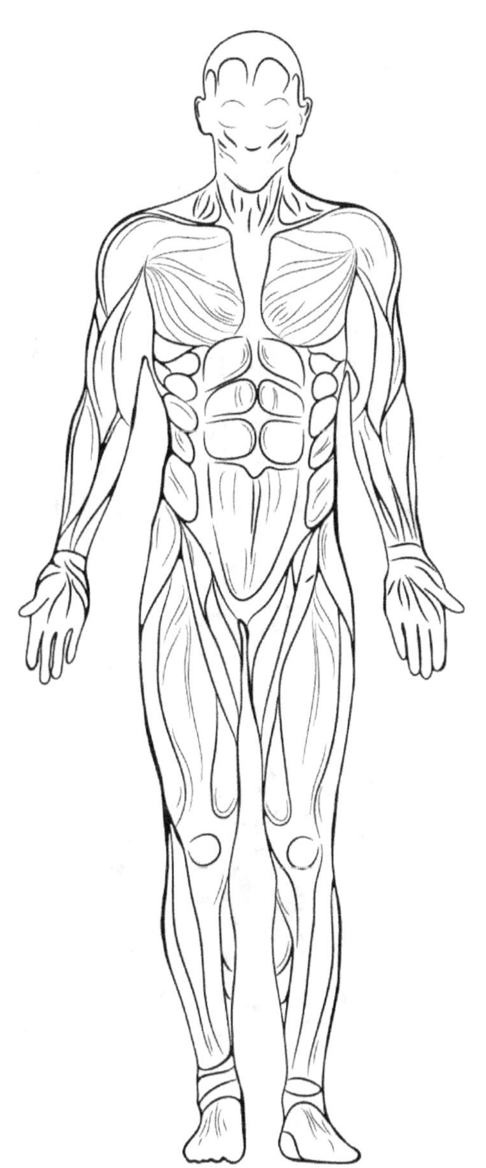

Eyes

The eyes allow us to see the world around us. They can distinguish between approximately 10 million different colors.

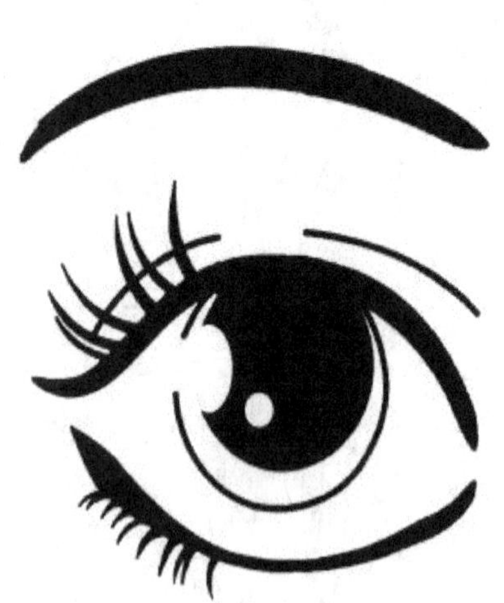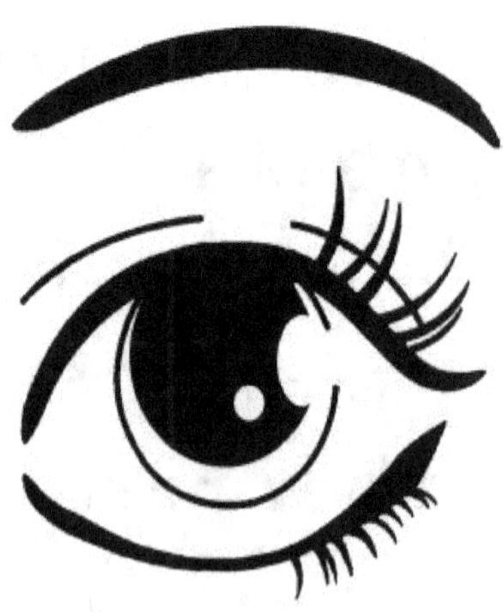

DNA

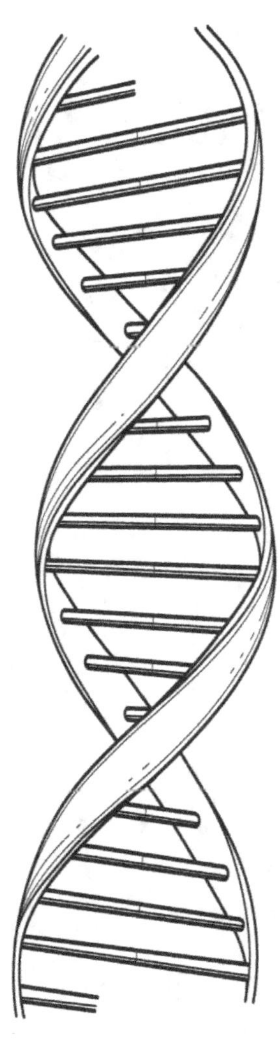

DNA (deoxyribonucleic acid) contains the genetic instructions that make each person unique. If all the DNA in your body was stretched out, it would reach the moon and back over 6,000 times!

FUN AND MIND-BOGGLING SCIENCE EXPERIMENTS

🚫 Please do not use any mentioned materials that may cause harm to you. It is important to have your parents present during any experiment.

Dancing Raisins

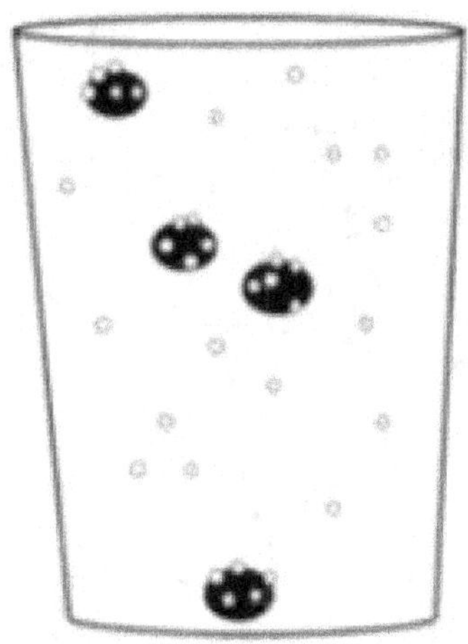

Fill a glass with carbonated water and drop some raisins into it. Watch as the raisins dance and float up and down due to the carbon dioxide bubbles attaching to them.

Magic Milk

Pour some milk into a shallow dish and add a few drops of different food coloring. Then, dip a cotton swab into dish soap and touch it to the milk. Watch as the colors swirl and mix together.

Homemade Volcano

Create a volcano by building a cone-shaped structure using modeling clay. Add baking soda into the volcano and pour vinegar mixed with red food coloring over it. Witness the eruption!

Egg in a Bottle

Place a hard-boiled egg on the mouth of a glass bottle. Light a piece of paper on fire and drop it into the bottle. Quickly cover the bottle with your hand and watch as the egg gets pulled inside due to the change in air pressure.

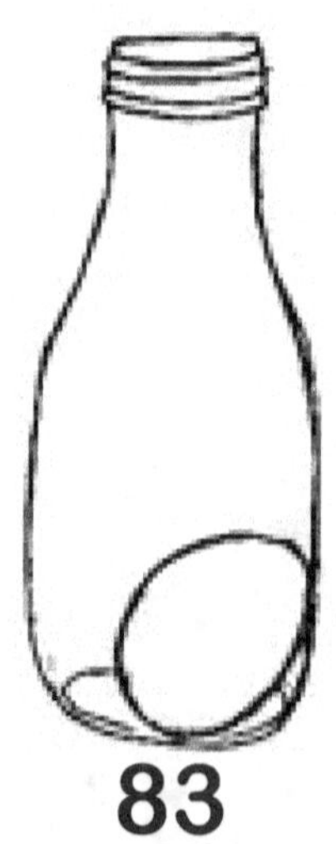

Invisible Ink

Use lemon juice or milk as invisible ink. Write a message on a piece of paper using a cotton swab dipped in the liquid. Let it dry, and when you want to reveal the message, hold the paper near a heat source, such as a light bulb.

Bending Water

Turn on a faucet to a slow stream and rub a comb or your hair against a woolen cloth. Bring the comb or hair close to the stream of water without touching it. Watch as the water bends towards the comb or hair.

Homemade Slime

Mix together equal parts of white school glue and liquid starch. Add food coloring or glitter for extra fun. Stir the mixture until it forms a slimy consistency. It's a gooey delight!

Balloon Rocket

Attach a long string or yarn between two chairs. Thread a straw onto the string and tape it securely. Blow up a balloon and attach it to the straw. Let go of the balloon, and watch it zoom along the string like a rocket!

Rainbow in a Glass

Fill a clear glass with water, leaving a little space at the top. Carefully pour different colors of food coloring into the glass, one at a time. Watch as the colors layer on top of each other, creating a beautiful rainbow effect.

Mentos and Soda Fountain

Drop a few Mentos candies into a bottle of soda and stand back! The reaction between the candies and the carbonation will cause a fizzy eruption, creating a soda fountain.

INCREDIBLE NATURAL PHENOMENA

Aurora Borealis (Northern Lights)

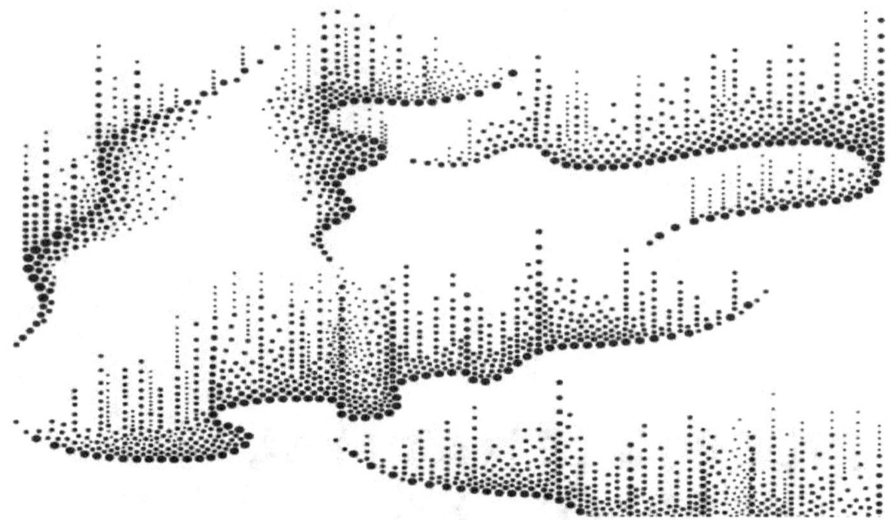

The Northern Lights are mesmerizing light displays that occur in the polar regions. They are caused by charged particles from the sun colliding with Earth's atmosphere, creating stunning colors and patterns in the night sky.

Bioluminescence

Bioluminescence is the emission of light by living organisms. It can be seen in various forms, such as glowing algae in the ocean or fireflies lighting up the night.

Rainbow

Rainbows occur when sunlight is refracted, or bent, by water droplets in the air. This bending of light creates the beautiful multicolored arc that we see after rain showers.

Geysers

Geysers are hot springs that periodically erupt with a column of boiling water and steam. The most famous geyser is Old Faithful in Yellowstone National Park, USA.

Tornadoes

Tornadoes are powerful and destructive rotating columns of air that extend from a thunderstorm to the ground. They are known for their high winds and funnel shape.

Solar Eclipse

A solar eclipse happens when the moon passes between the sun and Earth, temporarily blocking out the sun's light. This creates a dramatic celestial event where the sky turns dark during the day.

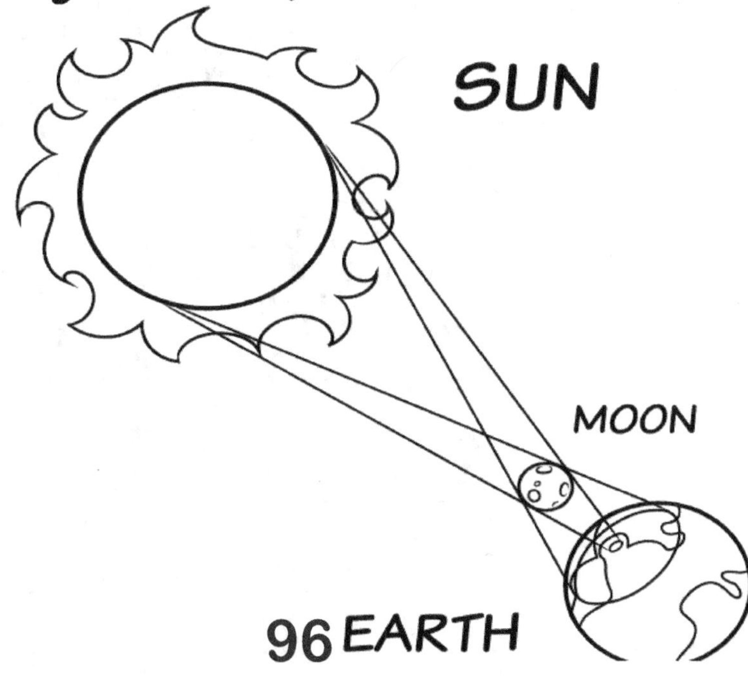

Waterfalls

Waterfalls are breathtaking natural wonders created when a river or stream flows over a steep drop or cliff. Examples include the majestic Niagara Falls and Angel Falls, the world's highest waterfall.

Sand Dunes

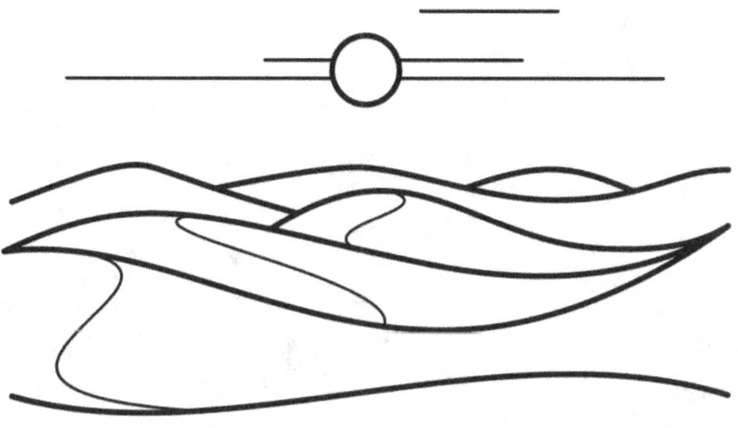

Sand dunes are large mounds of sand formed by wind or water movement. They can be found in deserts, coastal areas, and even on some planets like Mars.

Icebergs

Icebergs are massive chunks of ice that break off from glaciers and float in the ocean. They come in various shapes and sizes and can be found in polar regions.

Meteor Showers

Meteor showers occur when Earth passes through a trail of debris left by a comet. The debris burns up in the atmosphere, creating streaks of light known as shooting stars.

ENVIRONMENTAL CONSERVATION

Biodiversity

Biodiversity refers to the variety of plant and animal species on Earth. Did you know that Earth is home to millions of different species, ranging from tiny insects to enormous whales?

Habitat Restoration

Habitat restoration involves the rehabilitation and restoration of degraded ecosystems to their natural state. This may include reforestation, wetland restoration, coral reef rehabilitation, and other efforts to revive and protect critical habitats.

Sustainable Land Use

Sustainable land use practices aim to balance human activities with ecological processes. This includes sustainable agriculture, responsible forestry, land reclamation, and urban planning that prioritizes green spaces and preserves natural habitats.

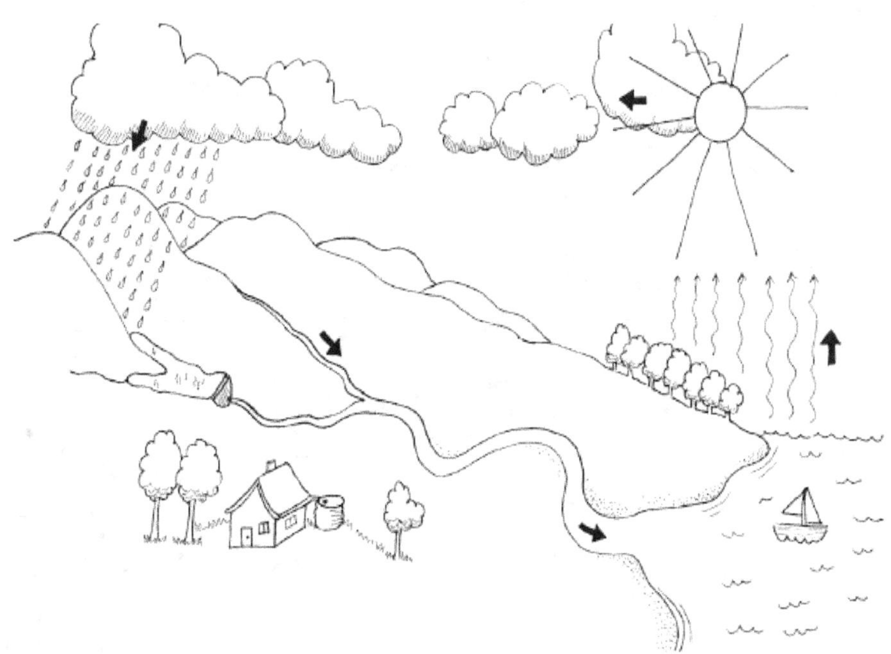

Water Resource Management

Water is a vital resource, and conservation efforts focus on sustainable water management. This includes protecting water sources, promoting water efficiency and conservation measures, implementing watershed management strategies, and addressing water pollution issues.

Sustainable Fisheries

Sustainable fisheries management ensures the long-term viability of fish populations while minimizing environmental impacts. It involves impelmenting fishing quotas, regulating fishing methods, protecting marine habitats, and promoting responsible fishing practices.

Pollution Control

Environmental conservation addresses pollution from various sources, including air, water, and soil. Efforts focus on reducing pollution through regulations, promoting cleaner technologies, waste management practices, and raising awareness about pollution prevention.

Climate Change Mitigation

Climate change is a pressing global issue, and conservation efforts play a crucial role in mitigating its impacts. This includes reducing greenhouse gas emissions, promoting renewable energy sources, adopting energy-efficient practices, and supporting climate change adaptation strategies.

Environmental Education and Awareness

Environmental education is essential for fostering a sense of responsibility and inspiring action. It involves raising awareness about environmental issues, promoting sustainable practices, and providing knowledge and skills to empower individuals and communities to make informed decisions.

Conservation Research and Monitoring

Scientific research and monitoring are crucial for understanding ecosystems, identifying threats to biodiversity, and evaluating the effectiveness of conservation measures. This includes ecological surveys, species monitoring, and studying the impacts of human activities on the environment.

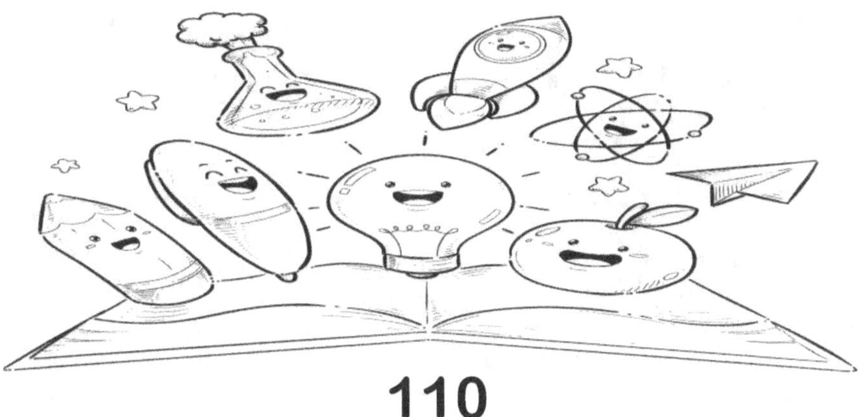

Conservation Policy and Advocacy

Environmental conservation relies on strong policies and regulations. Advocacy efforts involve influencing policymakers, promoting sustainable practices, supporting conservation initiatives, and engaging in public discourse to drive positive change.

Thank you!

www.ingramcontent.com/pod-product-compliance
Lightning Source LLC
Chambersburg PA
CBHW070813260726

48660CB00005B/1832